This journal belongs to:

_____

In loving memory of:

_____

ABOUT THE AUTHOR

Shaela Mauger and Harpermartin

Born and raised in Wagga Wagga regional New South Wales, Shaela has pursued her love of graphic design through university and began her career as a designer for a local printer.

Since becoming a mother, Shaela has fine tuned her passion for design towards what's most important to her: loved ones, and cherishing the time we have with them. Now, after half a decade of having her own design business, Shaela has launched Harpermartin — paying homage to her parents' family names — and this series of keepsake books, created to celebrate life and love in all its forms.

The series is available at www.harpermartin.com.au

ISBN 978-0-6482778-8-0

MISSING YOU

In memory of my loved one

Table of Contents

Photo pages throughout

In memory of my Dad, Greg x

PREFACE

I'm so sorry someone you love has died. My Dad died when I was five years old so I understand what it feels like to miss someone you love.

This book is designed for you to write down everything you love and miss about your loved one. Stick in your favourite photos, write letters, draw pictures, do what brings you comfort.

Never compare your grief to others because everyone grieves differently. This person was a very special part of your life and they always will be. This journal helps you put down on paper all the feelings and memories you hold dear.

I am thinking of you!

With love,

Shaela xx
Founder, Harpermartin

Full name:

Nickname:

Date and place of birth:

The day you died:

Your favourite number:

Your favourite colour:

Your favourite team:

Your favourite hobby:

Your favourite saying:

Your nickname for me:

My favourite memories...

Photos

Photos

All the things I loved doing with you...

I miss you saying and doing...

You taught me...

I wish you were here for...

If you were here today I would tell you this...

_____

_____

_____

_____

_____

_____

_____

_____

_____

_____

_____

_____

_____

A letter to you

All the things I remember about you now...

I love you to the moon and back
and more than all the stars in the sky

Big hugs from
www.harpermartin.com.au

www.ingramcontent.com/pod-product-compliance
Lightning Source LLC
Chambersburg PA
CBHW040258100426
42811CB00011B/1301